G000037228

I have an A+ teacher
who gives so much care...
I think my teacher's special,
no other can compare.

Dedicated to:

Mrs. Taylor
from
Lisa Middleton

© 1999 Havoc Publishing

Artwork © 1999 Linda Spivey
Under license from Penny Lane Publishing, Inc.
Text © 1999 Jill Lemming

ISBN 0-7416-1103-1

Published by Havoc Publishing
San Diego, California

Made in China

www.havocpub.com

Havoc Publishing
9808 Waples Street
San Diego, California 92121
U.S.A.

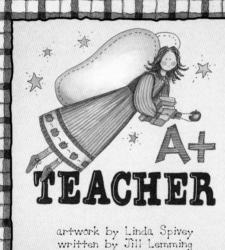

A+

TEACHER

artwork by Linda Spivey
written by Jill Lemming

A child is always nervous
when the first day of
school begins...
It takes a special
teacher to bring a smile
to each one of them.

Oo · Pp · Qq · Rr · Ss · Tt

Uu · Vv · Ww · Xx · Yy · Zz · 1 2 3

Instilling values in our
children, every boy and
every girl.

Writing II

ARITHMETIC

SPELLING

READING

Take time to tell a
teacher what a special
gift they've been...
Let them know your
appreciation, it may
bring a smile to them.

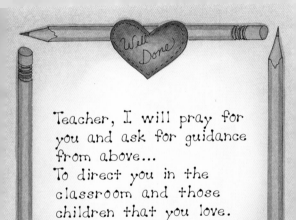

Well Done

Teacher, I will pray for
you and ask for guidance
from above...
To direct you in the
classroom and those
children that you love.

Aa Bb Cc Dd Ee Ff Gg Hh Ii Jj Kk Ll Mm Nn
Oo Pp Qq Rr Ss Tt Uu Vv Ww Xx Yy Zz 123

Many teachers that I've
had were special through
the years...
Each had their own way
of making dreams appear

AaBb Cc Dd Ee Ff Gg Hh Ii Jj Kk Ll Mm Nn
Oo Pp Qq Rr Ss Tt Uu Vv Ww Xx Yy Zz 123

I'm proud to have a
teacher who thinks the
world of me...
Teaching me to strive harder
to be the best I can be.

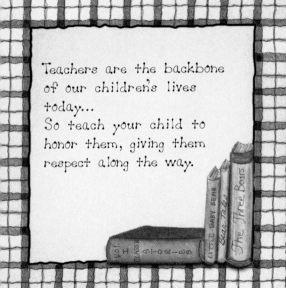

Teachers are the backbone
of our children's lives
today...
So teach your child to
honor them, giving them
respect along the way.

Our teachers should be

recognized for the

endless things they do...

It's more than a job they are doing, they make a difference for me and you.

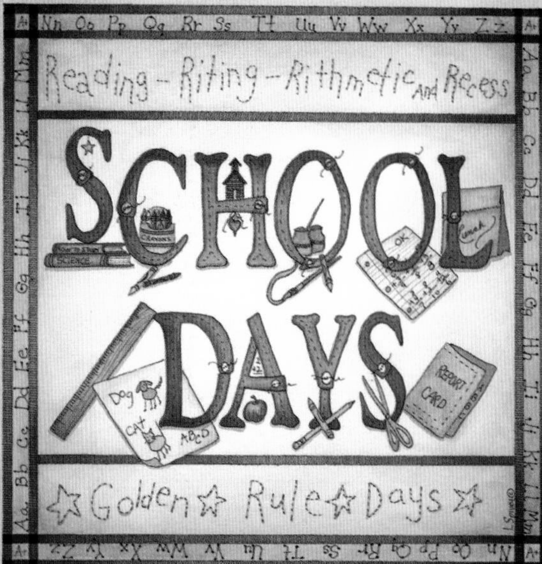
Reading - Riting - Rithmetic And Recess
SCHOOL
DAYS
SCIENCE
OK
Dog
CAT
ABCD
REPORT CARD
Golden Rule Days

Reading ~ Riting ~ Rithmetic And Recess

I've had some favorite
teachers that I respected
from the start...
one became a friend
who understood my heart.

☆ Golden ☆ Rule ☆ Days ☆

When a teacher values
children, it shows in
their attitude...
There's a sense of true
compassion, in what they
say and do.

Bless these special teachers,
give them grace to see
them through...
Bless the children they are
teaching and let love shine
upon them, too.

A teacher
should recall
how it feels
to be a child...
It helps when
they remember
to start each
day with a
smile.

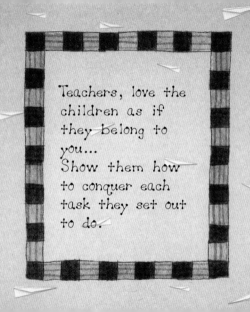

Teachers, love the children as if they belong to you...
Show them how to conquer each task they set out to do.

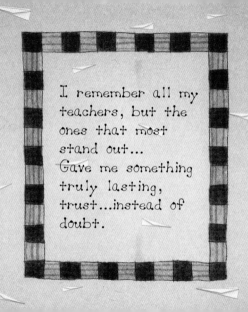

I remember all my teachers, but the ones that most stand out... Gave me something truly lasting, trust...instead of doubt.

Teachers
serve with wisdom
and help our
children shine...
They teach them
to keep searching
for the goals
they hope
to find.

A teacher earns a child's
respect by understanding
what they say...
By listening to their
problems, and being
mindful of them
each day.

Thank you for special
teachers who give their
lives each day...
In service to our
children, to show them
a better way.

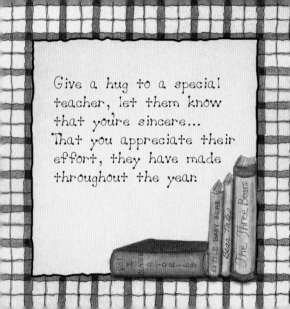

Give a hug to a special teacher, let them know that you're sincere... That you appreciate their effort, they have made throughout the year

Blessed teacher, friend
of mine, I'll keep your
memory near...
The lessons you have
taught me will remain in
my heart every year.

If I gave an apple for
every lesson that my
teachers taught to me...
I'd have to own an
orchard and grow each
one an apple tree.

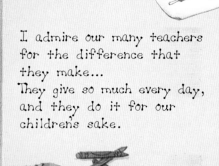

I admire our many teachers
for the difference that
they make...
They give so much every day,
and they do it for our
children's sake.

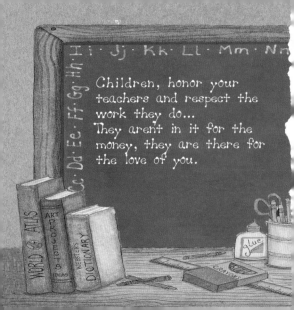

Ii · Jj · Kk · Ll · Mm · Nn

Children, honor your
teachers and respect the
work they do...
They aren't in it for the
money, they are there for
the love of you.

Do · Pp · Qq · Rr · Ss · Tt

Uu · Vv · Ww · Xx · Yy · Zz · 1 2 3

Grant peace to every teacher
who is serving every day...
Provide a safe environment
for our schools, for this
I pray.

Writing II

ARITHMETIC

SPELLING

READING

Well Done

Most teachers have a story about an extraordinary child... Each one holds special memories that makes their job worthwhile.

AaBb Cc Dd Ee Ff Gg Hh Ii Jj Kk Ll Mm Nn
Oo Pp Qq Rr Ss Tt Uu Vv Ww Xx Yy Zz 123

Bless my teacher who speaks
the words of truth to me...
Let my teacher be an inspiration
as I process and receive.

AaBb Cc Dd Ee Ff Gg Hh Ii Jj Kk Ll Mm Nn
Oo Pp Qq Rr Ss Tt Uu Vv Ww Xx Yy Zz 123

Teachers are my heroes for the
difference that they make...
For investing more than hours,
for giving more than they take.

Aa Bb Cc Dd Ee Ff Gg Hh

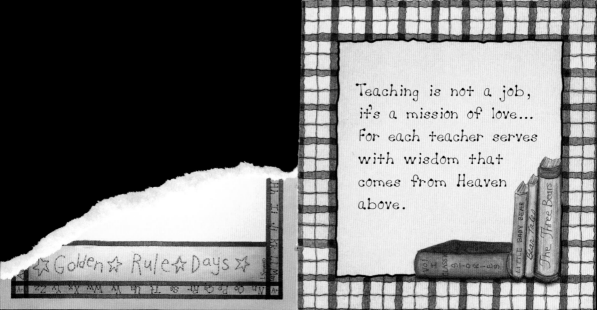

Teaching is not a job,
it's a mission of love...
For each teacher serves
with wisdom that
comes from Heaven
above.

it's

it's your attitude that shows.

The smartest kind of teacher
is the kind that truly knows,
it's not the clothes you're wearing

Reading - Riting - Rithmetic and Recess

Teacher, I must tell you,
I respected you from
the start...
For never giving up on me
when I failed to do
my part.

Teacher, I must tell you,
I respected you from
the start...
For never giving up on me
when I failed to do
my part.

The smartest kind of teacher
is the kind that truly knows...
It's not the clothes you're wearing
it's your attitude that shows.

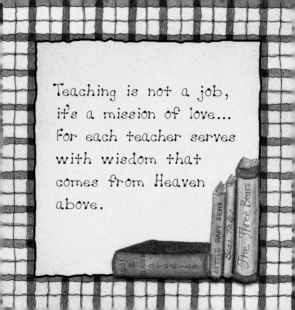

Nn Oo Pp Qq Rr Ss Tt Uu Vv Ww Xx Yy Zz

Reading - Riting - Rithmetic And Recess

Thanks to all our teachers
who have gone the extra
mile...
To bring knowledge to our
children, and loved it all
the while.

☆ Golden ☆ Rule ☆ Days ☆

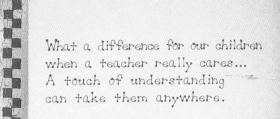

What a difference for our children
when a teacher really cares...
A touch of understanding
can take them anywhere.

Teachers come and teachers go
but are never far away...
They leave a lasting impression,
it's their attitudes that stay.

I'm blessed to have a teacher who has a gracious heart.

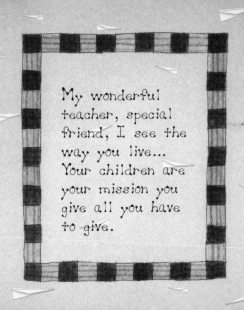

My wonderful
teacher, special
friend, I see the
way you live...
Your children are
your mission you
give all you have
to give.

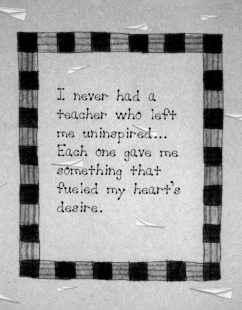

I never had a teacher who left me uninspired... Each one gave me something that fueled my heart's desire.

Teachers
should be
honored for
the lives left
in their hands...
We need to give
them credit
for their
"footprints" in
the sand.

The teachers that I've known have really seemed to care... They encouraged my potential with the knowledge that they shared.

Teachers are the leaders,
they are sustainers of
the truth...
They are gifted in their
thinking and respected
for what they do.

Take time to write a letter to a teacher in your past...
The one who made a difference teaching values that would last.

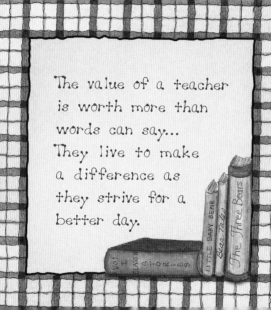

The value of a teacher
is worth more than
words can say...
They live to make
a difference as
they strive for a
better day.

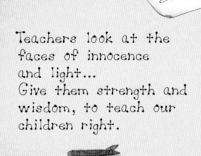

Teachers look at the
faces of innocence
and light...
Give them strength and
wisdom, to teach our
children right.

There are many special
teachers who deserve a
true reward...
for the hours they spend
planning for the children
they adore.

Oo · Pp · Qq · Rr · Ss · Tt

Uu · Vv · Ww · Xx · Yy · Zz · !?

Respect and consideration
should be part of every
school...
Our children need to learn
this important Golden Rule.

Writing

ARITHMETIC

SPELLING

READING

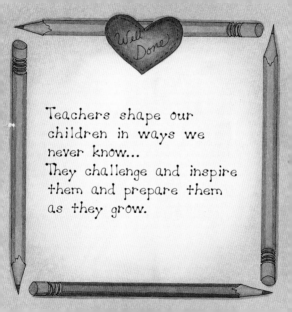

Well Done

Teachers shape our children in ways we never know... They challenge and inspire them and prepare them as they grow.

Aa Bb Cc Dd Ee Ff Gg Hh Ii Jj Kk Ll Mm Nn
Oo Pp Qq Rr Ss Tt Uu Vv Ww Xx Yy Zz 123

Reading, Writing, Arithmetic,
special field trips with the class...
Busy days for a teacher
that all go so fast.

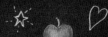

AaBb Cc Dd Ee Ff Gg Hh Ii Jj Kk Ll Mm Nn
Oo Pp Qq Rr Ss Tt Uu Vv Ww Xx Yy Zz 123

What makes a teacher special,
is the content of the heart...
It starts with a love for children,
what a beautiful way to start.

I said a thank you prayer for my teacher that I love...
Who shows faith in my ability and is my angel from above.

The teachers I remember
most even today can
make me smile...
They're the ones who
overlooked my faults and
loved me all the while.

Nn Oo Pp Qq Rr Ss Tt Uu Vv Ww Xx Yy Zz
Reading - Riting - Rithmetic And Recess
SCHOOL DAYS
CRAYONS
SCIENCE
OK
Lunch
Dog
CAT
ABCD
REPORT CARD
Golden ☆ Rule ☆ Days

Reading - Riting - Rithmetic and Recess

Blessed are the teachers
who strive to do their
best...
To educate our children,
while the parents do
the rest.

☆ Golden ☆ Rule ☆ Days ☆

Be kind to all your teachers
for they pay a hefty price...
They give themselves
unselfishly as your gift of
sacrifice.

My teacher
brings me
sunshine when
my sky is
dark and gray...
who teaches me
with kindness
and lights my
path each day.

Give our teachers
patience and hands
for doing good...
Working side-by-
side together, with
our children as
they should.

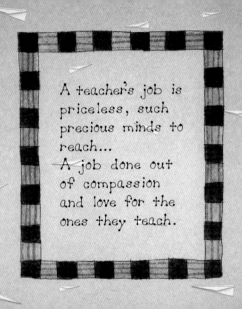

A teacher's job is
priceless, such
precious minds to
reach...
A job done out
of compassion
and love for the
ones they teach.

A truly
special teacher
is one who will
learn to see...
That our
children have
compassion
for all of
humanity.

A teacher puts no
boundaries when it
comes to children's
minds...
The sky is surely the
limit, imaginations an
endless climb.

You are my favorite teacher
who is a friend of mine...
your sweet and caring nature
is the reason for this rhyme.

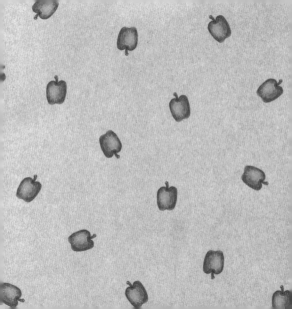